THE
CONNECTION FACTOR
FOR
LEADERS

UNLOCKING VALUE FROM YOUR STRATEGIC PARTNERS

CYNTHIA CHIRINDA

Wholeness
Incorporated
Publishing

The Connection Factor for Leaders
Unlocking Value from Your Strategic Partners
Copyright © 2025 by Cynthia Chirinda
Originally published in 2018
Revised and rebranded edition © 2025 Cynthia Chirinda
All rights reserved.

Scripture quotations, unless otherwise noted, are taken from the Holy Bible, King James Version (KJV).

Original Cover design by Tapiwa Kahonde.
Revised layout and design by Annie Nyamudzwadzuro
Published by Wholeness Incorporated
Harare, Zimbabwe

For coaching, consulting, author resources, or speaking engagements, visit:
www.cynthiachirinda.com
info@cynthiachirinda.com

ISBN: 978-0-7974-9759-7

CONTENTS

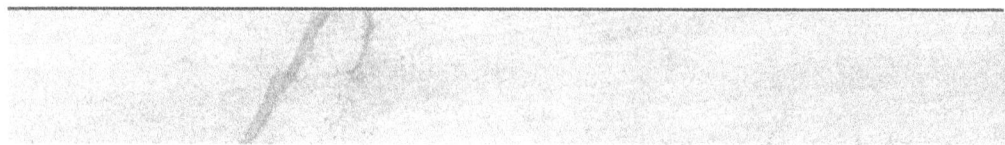

DEDICATION

To every leader and visionary who continues to courageously steer their ship with confidence in the face of turbulence and uncertainty. May your leadership be anchored in purpose, guided by wisdom, and graced with the strength to chart paths of transformation.

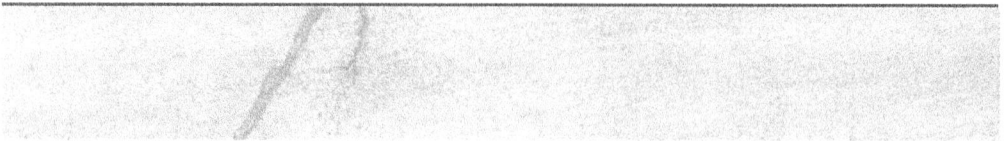

ACKNOWLEDGEMENTS

I would like to express my heartfelt gratitude to the many organisational leaders who have opened their corporate spaces to me, allowing for deep and transformative engagement. It has been a profound honour to journey alongside you in your seasons of growth, recalibration, and bold re-envisioning.

Through our shared work in strategy, organisational design, and human capital development, I have not only grown professionally but have come to deeply appreciate the immense responsibility and sacrifice that leadership demands. Especially in seasons marked by disruption and complexity, your resilience and willingness to lead with both head and heart have inspired me.

Thank you for trusting me to co-create, to listen, and to build with you. These pages are informed by your courage, your questions, your breakthroughs, and your unwavering commitment to lead with integrity.

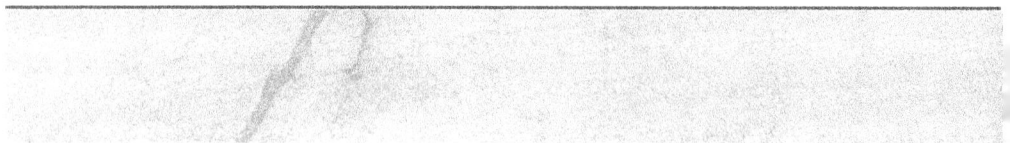

INTRODUCTION

As complexity deepens and connections multiply across every sphere, leadership is no longer defined by positional authority or the brilliance of an individual mind. It is defined by **relational intelligence**, **systems thinking**, and the ability to unlock value through **strategic partnerships**. Leadership is no longer about simply leading people—it is about **connecting purposefully**, stewarding influence, and activating the potential that lies within and around you.

We are witnessing a global call for leaders who are not only competent but also deeply **conscious**—leaders who embody empathy, navigate uncertainty with agility, and inspire trust-based collaboration in every sphere they serve. This is not a soft skill era—it is a **relational era**. And in this era, those who can cultivate, sustain, and leverage meaningful connections will be the ones who shape the future.

Over the years, I've had the privilege of working closely with leaders in corporate boardrooms, grassroots movements, government platforms, and ministry circles. One truth has remained consistent across all of these contexts: **relationships are the currency of leadership**. They influence culture, performance, innovation, and impact. The ability to build, nurture, and steward high-value relationships is not optional—it is essential.

But authentic connections don't happen by accident. They require intention, insight, and alignment. They require a leader to be **anchored in purpose** and **agile in engagement**. Many leaders form partnerships, but few know how to maximize their value. Others pursue stakeholder engagement without a clear framework for **relational strategy**, leaving outcomes to chance rather than design.

This book is my invitation to you to lead differently—to lead **from connection**. Not just social connection or networking, but purposeful, strategic, and **covenantal** connection. The kind that elevates trust, aligns vision, unlocks shared value, and multiplies impact.

In the pages ahead, we will explore how to:

- Rethink leadership through the lens of connection
- Develop agility and relational strategy in stakeholder engagement
- Identify and grow mutually empowering partnerships
- Navigate the terrain of relational leadership in governance, business, ministry, and civil society
- Build networks that are not just wide, but deep and sustainable

Whether you are an emerging leader, a seasoned executive, a policy influencer, or a spiritual shepherd, **The Connection Factor for Leaders** will challenge and equip you to steward your influence through relationships that matter.

This is leadership in motion—rooted in purpose, expressed through connection, and committed to transformation.

To Your Wholeness and Strategic Alignment,

Cynthia C

THE
CONNECTION FACTOR
FOR
LEADERS

UNLOCKING VALUE FROM YOUR STRATEGIC PARTNERS

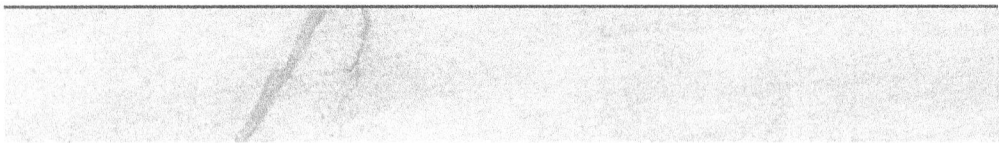

CHAPTER
ONE

—╫—

THE ESSENCE OF LEADERSHIP

"The greatest leader is not necessarily the one who does the greatest things. He is the one that gets the people to do the greatest things."
—RONALD REAGAN

REDEFINING LEADERSHIP FOR A NEW ERA

Leadership today is no longer confined to title, charisma, or control. It is about influence rooted in purpose, and intentionality expressed through connection. It is the ability to unlock value through meaningful relationships and steward that value toward lasting impact.

At its core, leadership is a relational force—a sacred responsibility to connect vision to people, potential to opportunity, and decision to transformation. In a volatile, uncertain, complex, and ambiguous (VUCA) world, effective leadership demands more than strategic brilliance. It calls for emotional maturity, relational intelligence, inner alignment, and spiritual depth.

We are living in a time marked not only by global crises, but by a leadership vacuum. We see it in governance, in business, in civil society, and even within faith communities. Titles abound, but transformative leadership is rare. Many have ascended to power but lost sight of the essence of true leadership: service, responsibility, vision, and connection.

What kind of leadership will shape the future? Not the loudest voice or the brightest star, but the most authentic, aligned, and relationally connected leader.

LEADING SELF BEFORE LEADING OTHERS

"Physician, heal thyself." Before leading others, leaders must first lead themselves.

Self-leadership is the cornerstone of sustainable influence. It involves mastering your thoughts, emotions, decisions, and habits. It is a daily discipline of alignment—between who you are, why you lead, and how you live.

Reflect deeply on these foundational questions:

- Who am I?
- Why am I here?
- Where am I going?
- How will I get there?
- What will be my legacy?

Leaders who live these questions lead with clarity, conviction, and coherence. They respond with intention rather than react from ego. They build trust by being the same person in private and public. Their leadership is not driven by applause, but by assignment.

Self-Awareness: The Gateway to Better Relationships

The quality of a leader's relationships is directly tied to the quality of their self-awareness. Without knowing yourself—your values, triggers, blind spots, and emotional landscape—you cannot meaningfully connect with or empower others.

Stephen Covey's Emotional Bank Account metaphor reminds us that every interaction is either a deposit or a withdrawal. Trust grows through deposits: empathy, consistency, transparency, and respect. When leaders withdraw too much through neglect or ego, relationships suffer.

Relational leadership starts with wholeness. Show up whole, and your team will mirror that authenticity.

Cultivating Leadership Intelligence

To lead with power and purpose, leaders must develop five core intelligences:

1. **Intrapersonal Intelligence**—*The Power of Knowing Yourself*
   - Deep self-awareness, reflection, and emotional alignment
   - "I am the greatest," Muhammad Ali declared. His inner dialogue shaped his outer world.

2. **Interpersonal Intelligence**—*The Capacity to Relate*
   - Empathy, listening, and emotional reading
   - Understanding others creates trust and moves people toward vision

3. **Intellectual Quotient (IQ)**—*Strategic Thinking*
   - Analysis, planning, and critical problem-solving
   - But intelligence without relationship limits influence

4. **Emotional Quotient (EQ)**—*Managing Self and Others*

- Emotional regulation and relational responsiveness
- In times of stress, EQ becomes a leader's compass

5. **Character Quotient (CQ)**—*Integrity in Action*
   - Values, ethics, and trustworthiness
   - Character sustains what charisma cannot. Without it, leadership collapses

WHY CHARACTER CANNOT BE COMPROMISED

A leader with high IQ and EQ but low CQ is dangerous: capable, yet unpredictable. Competence may gain influence, but only character sustains it.

Leaders must be trusted to do the right thing when no one is watching. Trust is the ultimate currency of leadership, and it is earned through consistency, humility, and integrity. Culture is not built by charisma—it is built by character in action.

FROM PERSONAL MASTERY TO ORGANIZATIONAL IMPACT

As a leader's influence expands, so must their focus. The move from self-mastery to organizational leadership involves shaping culture, designing systems, and empowering others.

Great organizational leaders:

- Build teams, not silos
- Empower others to grow and lead
- Align structure with purpose
- Balance people and performance
- Navigate change with faith and agility

They lead with an open hand, not a clenched fist. They steward people and resources with care, knowing that leadership is temporary, but legacy is eternal.

CASE STUDY: JACINDA ARDERN'S PEOPLE-FIRST LEADERSHIP

As Prime Minister of New Zealand, Jacinda Ardern modeled leadership marked by empathy, authenticity, and clarity. During crises such as the Christchurch mosque shootings and the COVID-19 pandemic, her approach centered the emotional and relational needs of her citizens.

Rather than posturing with authority, she communicated with vulnerability, inclusion, and confidence. Her leadership style reminds us that influence grows when trust deepens—and that character is as essential as policy.

FINAL REFLECTIONS

Leadership is not for the faint of heart. It requires a lifelong commitment to growth, healing, and humility. The world doesn't just need more leaders—it needs more *whole* leaders.

You cannot give what you do not have. Before you call others to excellence, cultivate it within yourself. Before you speak vision, align your inner world. Leadership begins with you.

The question is not, "Are you leading?" but "What kind of leader are you becoming?"

PRAYER AND DECLARATION FOR LEADERSHIP FORMATION

Lord,

Thank You for the sacred gift of leadership. I acknowledge that to lead others well, I must first be led by You and anchored in truth. Refine my heart, renew my mind, and align my life with purpose.

I declare:
> *I will lead with integrity, even when it is inconvenient.*
> *I will grow in wisdom, humility, and relational strength.*
> *I will be faithful with what I have been entrusted.*
> *I will build legacies that outlive me.*

Make me a leader who reflects Your heart. In Jesus' name, Amen.

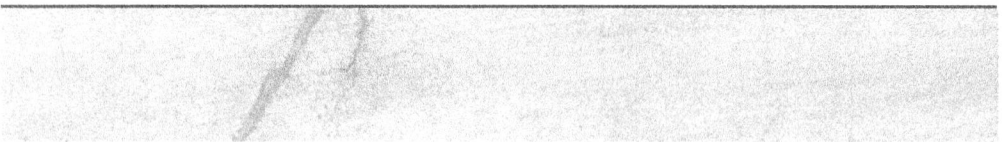

—#—

DEVELOPING LEADERSHIP AGILITY

"Leadership is about making others better as a result of your presence, and making sure that impact lasts in your absence."

—SHERYL SANDBERG

Leading at the Speed of Change

We are living in a time where the only certainty is uncertainty. Leadership today is being tested by the unrelenting pace of change—driven by digital disruption, socio-political complexity, global volatility, and shifting cultural expectations. For organizations to thrive, they require leaders who can not only anticipate change but move with it—confidently, creatively, and collaboratively.

This new era demands **Leadership Agility**—the capacity to think, decide, act, and adapt with both speed and wisdom.

Agile leaders do not wait for certainty; they lean into ambiguity with intention. They are grounded in purpose, yet fluid in approach. They can hold tension between paradoxes: structure and spontaneity, strategy and empathy, vision and listening.

What Does Leadership Agility Look Like?

Agile leaders are not simply multi-taskers or problem-solvers. They are **whole-brain thinkers** with an appetite for growth. They seek out challenges as learning opportunities, engage diverse perspectives, and are unafraid to revise their assumptions. They are comfortable being uncomfortable.

Here are some defining characteristics of agile leaders:

- Purpose-driven, yet open to evolving pathways
- Quick to act, but thoughtful in process
- Collaborative across disciplines and perspectives
- Deeply self-aware and constantly developing
- Adaptable without losing alignment or values

They do not shrink from difficult conversations or complex problems. Instead, they dive in with curiosity, knowing that deep learning happens in the discomfort zone.

CULTIVATING COGNITIVE AGILITY

Leadership agility starts with how we think. Every interaction, decision, or strategy begins in the mind. That's why mental flexibility is at the core of leadership effectiveness.

Ask yourself:

- What are my natural thinking styles—and how might they help or hinder me?
- Do I lean more toward analytical, relational, intuitive, or systematic approaches?
- What styles of thinking do I underuse or avoid?
- How often do I pause to reflect, recalibrate, and choose a different lens?

Too many leaders default to their thinking comfort zones. But in a world where change is non-linear, leaders must move fluidly across cognitive styles. This is not about abandoning your natural strengths—it's about **amplifying them with strategic stretch**.

STRETCHING BEYOND MENTAL BLIND SPOTS

Agile leaders know how to break out of their mental "autopilot." They ask for feedback. They seek opposing views. They create thinking time—not just reaction time.

For example, I schedule weekly thinking sessions—dedicated time to reflect, ideate, and recalibrate. Even 10 minutes a day can shift your neural patterns. Thinking is not a luxury; it is the engine of clarity, strategy, and reinvention.

Consider these practical questions for daily agility:
- What kind of thinking does this situation require?
- Where might my current perspective be too narrow?
- Who on my team sees this differently—and why?
- How can I build a habit of deliberate reflection?

Agility is not just about mental speed—it is about mental elasticity.

"Great leaders do not simply react—they zoom out, take
perspective, and then zoom back in with precision."

The **Leadership Agility Compass**, developed by *ChangeWise* through the
research of Bill Joiner, is a powerful graphic tool designed to help leaders
navigate complexity and drive effective action across any initiative.

LEADERSHIP AGILITY COMPASS

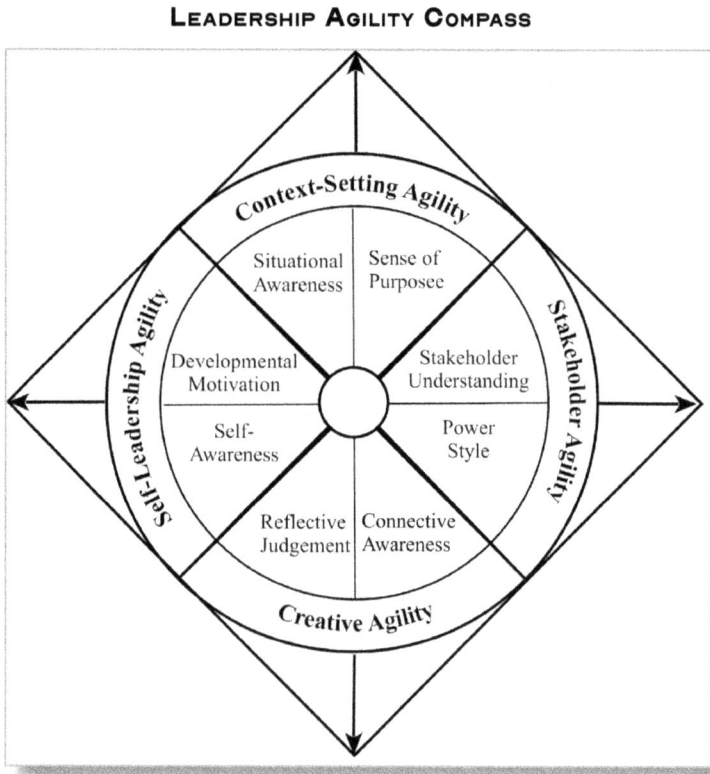

Source: Bill Joiner & ChangeWise (used with permission)

This model reveals four key "territories" every leader must attend to when
leading change, fostering team alignment, or driving innovation. The compass
guides leaders through intentional reflection and response across:

- **Context-Setting Agility**
- **Stakeholder Agility**
- **Creative Agility**
- **Self-Leadership Agility**

Each agility point represents a leadership muscle that, when exercised, enhances one's ability to lead effectively in fast-changing environments.

Introducing the Leadership Agility Compass

Developed by *ChangeWise* through the research of Bill Joiner, the **Leadership Agility Compass** provides a framework to navigate complexity with precision and perspective. It helps leaders engage four critical territories of influence in any leadership initiative:

1. **Context-Setting Agility**
   - Zoom out to understand the shifting environment.
   - Anticipate emerging challenges and align your initiative with strategic outcomes.
   - Ask: *Why does this matter now, and what outcomes are truly worth pursuing?*

2. **Stakeholder Agility**
   - Identify key stakeholders—those impacted by or needed for the initiative's success.
   - Step into their shoes. What do they see, feel, and fear?
   - Foster alignment through empathy and engagement, not coercion.

3. **Creative Agility**
   - Diagnose root issues. Explore bold, unconventional solutions.
   - Disrupt linear problem-solving with systems thinking and innovation.
   - Cross-functional collaboration becomes a tool for transformation.

4. **Self-Leadership Agility**
   - Reflect on how you show up. What are your biases, triggers, and blind spots?

- Practice self-observation before, during, and after key initiatives.
- Let feedback refine you. Leadership begins with inner alignment.

Each point on the compass is essential. Neglect one, and your leadership becomes imbalanced. Master all four, and your leadership becomes **transformational**.

THE DNA OF AGILE LEADERS

According to global research, agile leaders share these defining traits:

- **They Anticipate Change**
  They scan the horizon. They sense weak signals and adjust course before others even notice the shift. They don't react to change—they prepare for it.

- **They Generate Confidence**
  Agile leaders create psychological safety. Their teams feel empowered to experiment, fail fast, and learn forward. Trust, not fear, becomes the culture.

- **They Initiate Action**
  They don't wait for perfect conditions. They prototype, test, iterate. They align quickly around clear vision and cascade momentum through decisive action.

THREE LEVELS OF LEADERSHIP AGILITY

Research identifies three dominant levels of agility within organizations:

Agility Level	Orientation	Leadership Belief
Expert (45% of leaders)	Tactical, Problem-Solving	Respected for expertise and authority
Achiever (35% of leaders)	Strategic, Outcome-Focused	Motivates by aligning with larger goals
Catalyst (10% of leaders)	Visionary, Transformational	Inspires others to co-create change and grow capacity

The future belongs to **Catalyst Leaders**—those who build capacity, cultivate vision, and empower others to thrive. But it's a journey. Organizations must **support Expert and Achiever leaders to evolve**, stretch, and grow into new levels of agile leadership.

LEADERSHIP AGILITY IS A COLLECTIVE JOURNEY

As Bill Joiner aptly puts it, "Organizations must help many of their Achiever senior managers grow into the Catalyst level and many of their Expert middle managers develop to the Achiever level. This is a collective undertaking."

Leadership agility is not a solo pursuit. It is a **cultural investment**—one that multiplies impact across individuals, teams, and systems.

YOUR LEADERSHIP AUDIT

As you reflect on your current role and leadership influence, ask yourself:

- Where am I on the agility spectrum—Expert, Achiever, or Catalyst?
- How do I respond to ambiguity and pressure?
- What blind spots or defaults do I need to challenge?
- What territories of the Leadership Agility Compass do I neglect?
- How can I stretch myself—and empower others to grow with me?

Your ability to stay open, adaptable, and resilient in thought and action will determine your long-term effectiveness. In this era of accelerated change, **agility is not optional—it's the leadership superpower.**

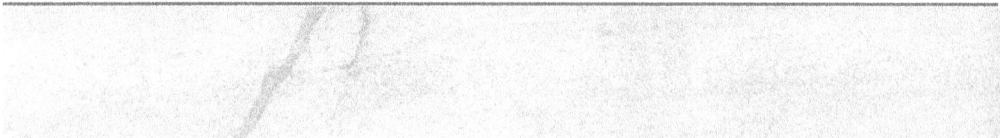

CHAPTER
THREE

RELATIONAL THINKING

*"Leadership is not about being in charge. It is about taking
care of those in your charge."*
—Simon Sinek

—‖—

*"Recognising the theoretical importance of relationships is no guarantee
that the relational aspects of situations, and the relational consequences of
decisions, will be recognised... Developing new tools to aid our perception and
analysis will therefore be essential in developing more effective leadership."*
—John Ashcroft et al., Relationships Foundation

THE CONNECTION FACTOR FOR LEADERS

WHAT LENS ARE YOU PUTTING ON?

I remember vividly the frenzy that hit our neighbourhood in the early 1980s when the British pop music outfit Five Star released their hit single "All Fall Down." With it came a trend—teenagers donning their denims and dark sunglasses with swagger and pride. I still recall the glee I felt when I "borrowed" my brother's shades for the first time. The world around me suddenly darkened—but it wasn't frightening. It was simply different. When I removed them, everything became familiar again—clear, light, and true.

That fleeting experience taught me something timeless: your perspective changes everything. In life, we may not control the variables—but we do control the lens through which we perceive and respond to them. One of the most dangerous lenses is the self-lens—a perspective that centers individualism, entitlement, and short-term gain. This lens filters out the collective good, limits empathy, and weakens our ability to build meaningful, sustainable systems.

To lead in today's complex world, we need to put on a different pair of lenses—the relational lens.

WHAT IS A RELATIONSHIP, REALLY?

Before diving into Relational Thinking, we must revisit the foundational question: What is a relationship?

A relationship is more than a one-off interaction. It is:

- A series of meaningful encounters with another (individual or group),
- Shaped by memory of the past and imagination of the future,
- Where both parties are known and knowable,
- Where the actions of one affect the other,
- Situated within a shared context.

This definition applies at every level—from friendships and family dynamics to teams, institutions, and international partnerships.

THE POWER AND PRACTICE OF RELATIONAL INTELLIGENCE

Leadership is fundamentally about relationships. In a world of increasing complexity and rapid change, leaders who cultivate relational intelligence not only foster more engaged teams but also drive more sustainable results.

Relational Intelligence (RI) refers to the ability to successfully connect with people and build strong, authentic relationships. It's not just a 'soft skill'—it's a strategic imperative. Leaders with high RI:

- Listen actively
- Empathize genuinely
- Communicate clearly
- Perceive the spoken and the unspoken

They understand that people are not simply cogs in a machine but carriers of purpose, potential, and perspective.

DIMENSIONS OF RELATIONAL LEADERSHIP

To lead relationally means to invest in the following:

- **Trust**: Built through consistency, honesty, vulnerability, and follow-through.
- **Respect**: Seeing the inherent value in others.
- **Empathy**: Understanding and responding to others' emotional landscapes.
- **Collaboration**: Encouraging shared goals and constructive conflict resolution.
- **Communication**: Clear, timely, and truthful exchanges that build understanding.

Relational leaders recognize that relationships are the bridges over which vision, strategy, feedback, and change travel. Without strong bridges, even the best ideas fall into the abyss.

RELATIONAL THINKING DEFINED

Relational Thinking is a paradigm that centers the quality and structure of relationships in all spheres of life—personal, organizational, and societal.

"It is a paradigm shift where we view everything through
a relational lens, speak with relational language, and use
relational tools to reach relational goals."
—RELATIONSHIPS GLOBAL (UK)

Unlike the world's transactional mindset—"use people, love things"—relational thinking invites us to love people and use things. It advocates a shift from materialism and individualism toward sustainable human connection.

A Relational Leader demonstrates:

- Servanthood
- Teamwork
- Authentic care
- Transparency
- Commitment to personal and collective growth

TRANSACTIONAL VS. TRANSFORMATIONAL RELATIONSHIPS

Too often, leaders fall into the trap of transactional leadership—interacting with others only to get things done. While results are important, transformational leadership recognizes that investing in people creates a ripple effect of growth, innovation, and trust.

- **Transactional mindset**: "What can I get from this person?"
- **Transformational mindset**: "How can I add value to this person?"

This mindset shift moves leadership from manipulation to empowerment, and from short-term gain to long-term significance.

THE RELATIONAL PROXIMITY® FRAMEWORK

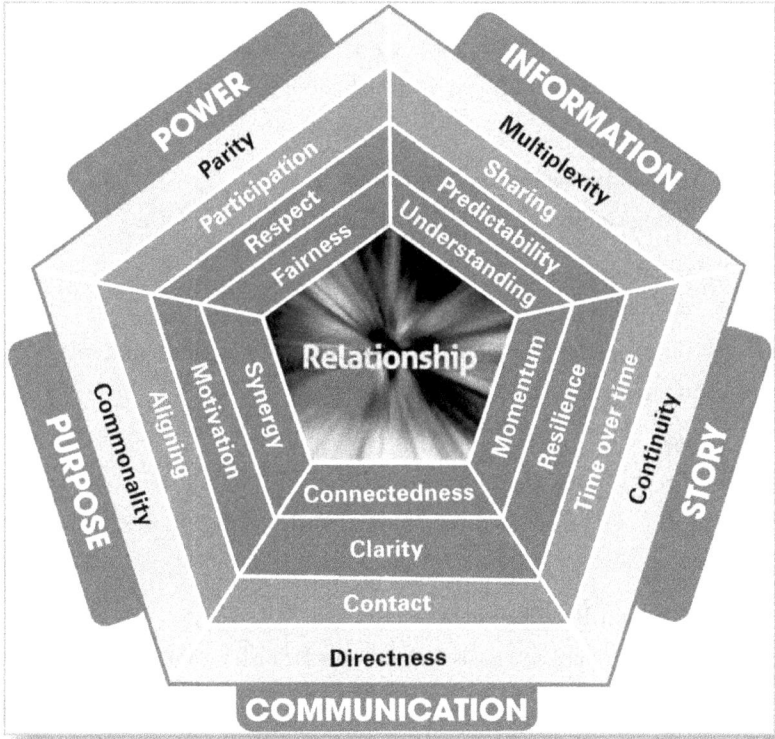

One of the most impactful models for understanding relational dynamics is the **Relational Proximity® Framework**, developed through years of multidisciplinary research. Relationships Foundation was responsible for the development of the model of Relational Proximity which has now been transferred to the profit-making company **Relational Analytics** as the Relational Proximity ® Framework.

The principle behind the model, and its practical usefulness, is the belief that the quality of relationships has a huge impact on business outcomes, productivity and sustainability, and impacts social harmony and personal wellbeing.

It explores five key dimensions of relational health:

1. **Communication (Contact)**
   - Directness, Clarity, Contact
   - Healthy relationships require timely, honest, and meaningful dialogue.

2. **Story (Time)**
   - Continuity, Resilience, Momentum
   - Strong connections have shared history and future focus.

3. **Information**
   - Multiplicity, Sharing, Predictability
   - Thriving relationships are marked by open, accessible, and reciprocal knowledge.

4. **Power**
   - Parity, Participation, Respect
   - Relational leaders steward power ethically and inclusively.

5. **Purpose**
   - Commonality, Alignment, Motivation
   - Aligned values and goals foster deep relational meaning.

Together, these dimensions generate **relational proximity**—a sense of closeness, trust, and mutual value.

Relational Thinking Is Sustainable Thinking

Whether leading families, teams, businesses, or nations—relationships matter. They are not a "soft" aspect of leadership; they are a critical asset. In strategic and operational contexts, strong relationships:

- Enhance culture and cohesion
- Foster trust and innovation
- Influence retention and loyalty
- Shape reputation and relevance

Relational disconnection is one of the leading causes of dysfunction in teams and communities. Adopting a relational lens promotes trust, fairness, mutual accountability, and belonging.

Faith-Inspired Relational Leadership

From a biblical perspective, relational leadership mirrors God's heart. Jesus modeled relational thinking in how He saw people, paused for them, engaged deeply, and empowered them.

The call to love your neighbour as yourself is not just a moral obligation— it is a leadership strategy that transforms systems. As Proverbs 27:17 reminds us, "As iron sharpens iron, so one person sharpens another."

A Call to Shift Our Thinking

The greatest tragedy of our time is not just broken systems—but broken ways of seeing. We've learned to measure success by profit, prestige, or performance— yet neglected to nurture the very relationships that sustain them.

But today, you have a choice.

Choose to see differently.

Choose to lead relationally.

When you commit to thinking relationally, you begin to build:
- Stronger families
- More cohesive teams
- Sustainable partnerships
- Healthier organizations
- Flourishing communities
- A life and legacy rooted in wholeness

REFLECTION QUESTIONS

1. What lens are you currently using to view your work, team, or life?
2. Which area of relational proximity do you need to grow in most— communication, story, information, power, or purpose?

3. Who are the key people you are called to intentionally connect with in this season?
4. What behaviours or habits are helping—or hindering—your relational leadership?
5. What one decision could you make today to move toward more relational leadership?

To your wholeness and impact.

Cynthia C

—‖—

RELATIONSHIPS THAT EVERY
LEADER NEEDS

"The measure of a man's greatness is not the number of servants he has, but the number of people he serves."

—JOHN C. MAXWELL

THE POWER OF STRATEGIC CONNECTION

Meaningful relationships that come from real interaction are the basis of success. Connecting effectively is therefore an important personal and business leadership skill. A powerful catalyst for inspiring creative breakthroughs is to guide people to connect with one another first, before trying to solve a problem. When people connect—when they are on the same wavelength, attuned, and in rapport—they are much better at generating and implementing new ideas.

Contemporary research also shows that connectedness with others is a strong predictor of longevity, health, and happiness. In a world driven by complexity and change, leaders who cultivate relational depth gain more than emotional rewards—they gain strategic advantage.

If you find yourself working harder than ever but not getting the results you want, perhaps more hard work is not the answer. Leaders today need to do more than simply work hard; they need leverage. That leverage comes from building relationships.

BUILDING HUMAN PARTNERSHIPS

According to Paul Fein, an organizational development consultant and certified life coach, "Leadership is more than just a science, more than just an art, and more than just a craft. Leadership is founded on human chemistry—the ability for a leader to look inward and become fully self-aware, and the ability for a leader to look outward and to build an understanding of others."

Leaders need to meet the needs of diverse people, including employees, colleagues, shareholders, external customers, and personal connections. This means communicating openly, listening more, being honest, having a dynamic vision, and being accountable. Compassion, empathy, emotional and social intelligence are critical to building lasting relationships.

Fein outlines six components for building strong human partnerships:

1. **Connection and Direction**

   Provide clarity, articulate goals, and translate vision into actionable steps. Motivate others through dynamic, purpose-driven communication.

2. **Empowerment and Ownership**

   Model responsibility and accountability. Empower employees to participate in strategy and take ownership of outcomes.

3. **Recognition and Appreciation**

   Show gratitude and celebrate individual and organizational successes. Use kindness to build loyalty and satisfaction.

4. **Innovative Culture and Environment**

   Encourage learning, tolerate risk, and model vulnerability. Create win-win solutions and support long-term growth.

5. **High Levels of Honesty and Transparency**

   Foster trust through consistency, humility, and truthfulness. Inspire positive behavior through authentic leadership.

6. **Relationships and Partnerships**

   Create cross-functional relationships, listen deeply, and build collaborative teams. Avoid judgment and lead with curiosity.

Five Foundational Relationship Domains for Every Leader

To lead well, you must lead connected. Here are five core relational domains every leader must nurture:

1. **Relationship with Self**

   Self-awareness is foundational. Monitor your emotions and reactions. Develop a daily rhythm of reflection and renewal. Without personal wholeness, professional leadership becomes hollow.

2. **Relationship with Support System**

   Nurture personal support systems—family, friends, mentors. These individuals provide emotional and spiritual balance. They remind you who you are beyond your title.

3. **Relationship with Your Team**
   Model vulnerability, accountability, and openness. Lead with humility and empower others through compassion and curiosity. Relationships are the soil where trust and innovation grow.

4. **Relationship with Stakeholders**
   Identify key stakeholders, understand their needs, and communicate in their preferred style. Build mutual trust and respect. Show them they matter beyond the metrics.

5. **Relationship with Authority or Clients**
   Whether it's a boss, board, investor, or customer—invest time and effort into this vital relationship. Build a bond based on integrity, trust, and clear communication.

CASE STUDY:

NELSON MANDELA'S LEGACY OF RELATIONAL LEADERSHIP

Nelson Mandela understood that enduring leadership is built on the foundation of relationships. During and after his imprisonment, he nurtured relationships across divides—with former enemies, political opponents, grassroots leaders, and international partners. His leadership style was marked by grace, empathy, and inclusivity.

Mandela famously stated, "If you want to make peace with your enemy, you have to work with your enemy. Then he becomes your partner."

His ability to reconcile, relate, and build bridges transformed South Africa's destiny. He remains a global example of what it means to lead not just with policy, but with presence.

FINAL REFLECTIONS

Relationships are the true currency of leadership. More than hard work, it is the quality and intentionality of your relationships that determine your success. Evaluate yourself in each of these five areas. Identify your strengths, acknowledge your gaps, and take steps to nurture every relationship with purpose.

In a world driven by results, remember that behind every goal is a group of people working toward it. Value people. Ask questions. Listen deeply. Build trust. Communicate with clarity.

When you invest in your relationships, you multiply your leadership impact—not just in the workplace, but in every area of life.

PRAYER AND DECLARATION FOR RELATIONAL LEADERSHIP

Lord,

Thank You for the gift of relationships. Teach me to lead with empathy, to listen more deeply, and to honor those You have placed in my path. Help me to be a safe place for growth, and a builder of bridges across differences.

I declare:

- ▷ *I will steward my relationships with wisdom and grace.*
- ▷ *I will build trust through integrity, presence, and truth.*
- ▷ *I will be a leader who unites, not divides.*
- ▷ *I will value people above performance and connection above control.*

May my leadership reflect Your love, and may my relationships speak louder than my title.

In Jesus' name, Amen.

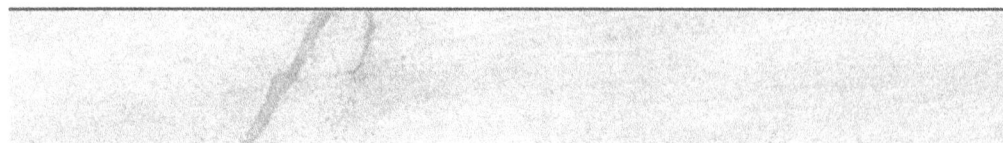

―✠―

KNOWING, ENGAGING AND
MANAGING YOUR STAKEHOLDERS

*"To keep everyone invested in your vision, you have to back up a little
bit and really analyze who the different stakeholders are and what they
individually respond to."*

— ALAN STERN

LEADING WITH STAKEHOLDER WISDOM

Leadership in today's interconnected world requires a panoramic view—one that includes not only internal teams or visible investors, but also the wide-ranging web of individuals and communities who are affected by our decisions. As leaders, we are not only strategists; we are stewards of relationships and influence.

Servant leadership, as articulated by Robert K. Greenleaf, calls us to ask: *"Do those served grow as persons? Do they become healthier, wiser, freer, more autonomous, more likely themselves to become servants?"* When leaders adopt this mindset, both people and organizations flourish. Studies by Sendjaya and Sarros affirm that servant leadership principles are practiced by some of the world's most resilient and high-performing organizations.

DO YOU REALLY KNOW YOUR STAKEHOLDERS?

A stakeholder is anyone with a vested interest in your leadership, work, or organization. Too often, leaders focus narrowly—on investors, clients, or boards—and neglect the broader network. Kingdom-minded leadership requires a wider lens: seeing beyond immediate outcomes to long-term value creation through relationship.

CATEGORIES OF STAKEHOLDERS

Invested Stakeholders include:

- Investors: Shareholders, owners, public investors
- Employees: Paid staff, volunteers
- Partners: Contractors, joint ventures, vendors

Impacted Stakeholders include:

- Communities: Physical, digital, or industry-based
- Social Causes: Environmental or societal causes touched by your mission

- Families: Those affected by your workplace culture or decisions

STAKEHOLDER CIRCLES BY CONTEXT

Depending on your leadership domain, stakeholder groups may vary:

- **Business:** Investors, government, customers, employees, communities
- **Nonprofit:** Donors, clients, volunteers, partners, staff, local communities
- **Church:** Congregation, ministries, staff, neighborhood, outreach partners
- **Politics:** Donors, constituents, agencies, communities, businesses

STAKEHOLDER MAPPING: A 3-STEP APPROACH

Step 1: Identification

Make a comprehensive list. Use these prompts:

- Who influences or is influenced by your initiative?
- Who controls key decisions or resources?
- Who might resist, challenge, or champion your vision?

Categorize them:

- Owners (shareholders, founders)
- Customers or service recipients
- Employees and teams
- Competitors, suppliers, networks
- Community organizations and advocacy groups
- Government and policy influencers
- Faith-based and civil society voices

Step 2: Prioritisation

Use the 2x2 Stakeholder Influence/Interest Grid:

- **High Influence / High Interest**—Key Players: Engage deeply and regularly
- **High Influence / Low Interest**—Keep Satisfied: Targeted updates
- **Low Influence / High Interest**—Keep Informed: Consistent communication
- **Low Influence / Low Interest**—Monitor and respond as needed

Step 3: Understand Their Need

Stakeholders have different expectations:

- Employees seek purpose and support
- Customers want consistent quality and reliability
- Investors desire growth and return on trust
- Communities value social impact and transparency
- Regulators need ethical compliance and cooperation

MAKING STAKEHOLDER ENGAGEMENT MEANINGFUL

Stakeholder engagement has evolved from a check-box task into a transformational tool. It's about:

- Building **mutual trust** through listening and responsiveness
- Embedding **stakeholder voices** into decision-making processes
- Creating value that transcends the transactional

In a Kingdom leadership context, this means viewing stakeholders not as means to an end, but as people with worth, dignity, and a role in your shared mission.

Effective engagement requires:

- Taking a holistic view of influence and responsibility
- Prioritizing dignity, justice, and transparency
- Being quick to listen and slow to presume

CASE STUDY:
PATAGONIA'S PURPOSE-DRIVEN STAKEHOLDER STRATEGY

Outdoor apparel company Patagonia has gained global recognition for embedding environmental and social stewardship into its business model. Their stakeholder model includes:

- Customers: Invited into sustainability partnerships
- Employees: Empowered with ownership and ethical culture
- Communities: Supported through environmental grants and activism
- Planet: Considered a primary stakeholder through bold ecological commitments

Their bold decision to transfer ownership of the company to a climate trust exemplifies values-driven stakeholder stewardship. Patagonia leads not only in profit but in principle.

FINAL REFLECTIONS

Stakeholder leadership is not just about management—it is about stewardship. Every person affected by your leadership is a trust. Every interaction is an opportunity to deepen impact.

Ask yourself:

- Where can I build deeper trust?
- Which stakeholder relationships need restoration?
- How can I shift from transaction to transformation?

When you engage stakeholders with intentionality, humility, and vision, you expand the reach and resilience of your leadership.

PRAYER AND DECLARATION FOR STAKEHOLDER WISDOM

Father, Thank You for entrusting me with influence and responsibility. Open my eyes to see every stakeholder as someone created in Your image. Help me to steward every relationship with integrity and love.

I declare:

I will lead with awareness, empathy, and justice.

I will serve with intention and build bridges of trust.

I will value voices that challenge, not just those that cheer.

I will build systems that reflect Your heart for people and purpose.

Empower me to lead beyond myself—and to build a legacy that uplifts everyone entrusted to my care.

In Jesus' name, Amen.

---||---

MAKING STRATEGIC
PARTNERSHIPS WORK

"If you want to go fast, go alone. If you want to go far, go together."
—AFRICAN PROVERB

THE STRATEGIC POWER OF PARTNERSHIP

From ancient alliances to modern joint ventures, partnerships have always shaped human progress. In today's interconnected, innovation-driven, and resource-sensitive world, **strategic partnerships are not just advantageous—they are essential**.

Organizations across every sector are learning that they can no longer thrive in isolation. Whether the goal is to expand reach, drive innovation, reduce costs, or increase agility, strategic partnerships offer a way to do more with others than one can alone.

According to a 2014 PwC CEO Survey, over 80% of US CEOs planned to pursue strategic partnerships—but only 65% of those efforts succeeded. The question is: **What distinguishes thriving partnerships from those that fail?**

WHAT MAKES A PARTNERSHIP STRATEGIC?

A strategic partnership is defined by:

1. **Independence with Interdependence**
    Partners remain autonomous while relying on each other to reach shared goals.

2. **Shared Risk and Reward**
    Both parties contribute, both parties benefit.

3. **Strategic Contribution**
    Each partner brings unique value to achieve a joint objective.

Examples include:

- Joint ventures
- R&D or innovation alliances
- Shared service or distribution agreements
- Strategic sourcing or equity-based collaborations

Common Pitfalls of Strategic Partnerships

More than half of all partnerships fail due to:

- **Underinvestment**: Lack of leadership support or misaligned resource allocation
- **Overreach**: Conflict over IP, customer ownership, or competition boundaries
- **Misalignment**: Clashing values, unclear roles, or weak value propositions

The Five Essentials for Strategic Partnership Success

1. **Strategize**

   Anchor your partnership strategy in your larger organizational mission. Clarify how the collaboration adds value.

   Case in Point: Nestlé's partnership-led innovation model included alliances with universities and startups, revitalizing product pipelines.

2. **Search, Screen, and Select**

   Scan broadly across sectors. Look for complementary capabilities and cultural alignment, not just brand reputation.

   Case in Point: NetApp and Cisco created "FlexPod" by aligning strengths in infrastructure and cloud services.

3. **Structure Thoughtfully**

   Choose the right structure:

   - **Non-equity alliances** for flexibility
   - **Joint ventures** for deeper integration

   Negotiate clearly on:

   - IP rights
   - Role distribution
   - Governance models
   - Conflict resolution and exit terms

   Case in Point: Starbucks' successful venture with Tata in India emerged after earlier failed attempts. Cultural sensitivity, supply chain clarity, and joint governance were prioritized.

4. **Start and Stabilize**

Early phases can be fragile. Use **interest-based negotiation** and conflict resolution tools to:
- Focus on shared outcomes
- Separate people from problems
- Establish joint communication protocols

Support the partnership with:
- Clear onboarding and shared tools
- Executive sponsorship
- Cross-organizational communication

5. **Study and Steer**

Form an Alliance Management Office or dedicated liaison team to:
- Track performance and outcomes
- Share learnings across units
- Institutionalize best practices

Case in Point: Eli Lilly's Office of Alliance Management has become a benchmark in pharma partnerships.

TYPES OF STRATEGIC PARTNERSHIPS

Type	Description
Marketing Partners	Joint campaigns, brand collaborations
Financial Partners	Accountants, advisors, investors
Suppliers	Co-development, exclusive access, improved terms
Technology Partners	Custom tools, system integration, digital innovation
Funding Alliances	Joint grant proposals or philanthropic projects
Cost/Resource Sharing	Shared infrastructure, admin, or operational support

Classifying by Structure:

Structure	Characteristics
Collaboration	Informal cooperation, shared interests
Strategic Alliance	Shared decision-making and goals
Integration	Joint ventures, mergers, or blended operations
Grant Match	In-kind resources exchanged for funding
Cost-Sharing	Equal contributions toward shared initiatives

KEY LESSONS IN SUSTAINING PARTNERSHIPS

1. **Invest in Relationship Management**

   Assign dedicated partnership managers who track both technical and relational health.

2. **Develop Shared Metrics**

   Define success together: include collaboration health, cultural alignment, and measurable impact.

3. **Prepare for Transitions**

   Partnerships have life cycles. Reassess often. Plan for evolution, renewal, or closure with integrity.

CASE STUDY: STARBUCKS AND TATA

Starbucks' entry into India faced early delays due to cultural and regulatory complexities. Their eventual partnership with Tata Group succeeded due to:

- Shared values around ethical sourcing and sustainability
- Clear governance structures
- Mutual respect and cultural adaptation

This joint venture now stands as a blueprint for navigating partnerships across diverse contexts.

FINAL REFLECTIONS: PARTNERSHIP AS A MINDSET

Strategic partnerships are not just contracts—they are relationships. They require:

- Trust
- Transparency
- Mutual value
- A long-term view

When done right, they unlock innovation, expand impact, and multiply influence.

"Trust becomes the new currency. Relationship is the new infrastructure. Partnership is the new strategy."

PRAYER AND DECLARATION FOR PARTNERSHIP WISDOM

Heavenly Father,

Thank You for the gift of collaboration. I acknowledge that I am not called to build alone. Guide me in forming relationships that honour You and serve others with excellence.

I declare:

> *I will pursue partnerships that are built on trust and mutual purpose.*
> *I will communicate clearly, serve humbly, and resolve conflict with grace.*
> *I will steward every alliance with wisdom and integrity.*
> *I will see people, not just possibilities.*

Help me walk in alignment with Your heart and build partnerships that reflect Your Kingdom.

In Jesus' name, Amen.

---||---

FOSTERING CONNECTEDNESS
IN THE CHURCH

"Behold, how good and how pleasant it is for brethren to dwell together in unity!"

—PSALM 133:1

THE CHURCH: A SACRED SPACE FOR CONNECTION

Human beings are created for relationships. All of us need others in order to thrive. The Church has long been a key institution for fostering belonging, care, and spiritual connection. It offers a sacred space where people receive warmth, encouragement, assistance, and affirmation—especially in times of distress.

To be effective in ministry, church leaders must foster relational and spiritual connectedness across all levels. The power of belonging cannot be underestimated. When people are known, valued, and spiritually nurtured, the church becomes a sanctuary of healing, growth, and purpose.

Benefits of spiritual and relational connectedness include:

- A sense of identity
- The ability to love and be loved
- Greater happiness and wellbeing
- Affirmation of self-worth
- A network of support during trials
- Exposure to diverse perspectives that enrich spiritual growth

ASSIMILATION BEST PRACTICES IN THE CHURCH

For believers, the Church is not a building—it's a people. Whether someone is a lifelong member or a first-time visitor, their spiritual wellbeing matters. Assimilating people into the life of the church is vital for cultivating true discipleship and sustained involvement.

Churches should focus on three essential pathways:

1. **Fellowship**

   Nurture authentic connection through events, shared meals, small groups, and hospitality. Relationship is the soil in which spiritual growth takes root.

2. **Discipleship**

   Offer opportunities for mentoring, Bible study, and spiritual formation.

Discipleship rooted in relationship creates accountability and spiritual maturity.

3. Service

Help individuals discover and activate their spiritual gifts. People feel most connected when they are empowered to contribute meaningfully. When people find a place where they truly belong, the church becomes a living, breathing body of Christ that ministers effectively.

The Church and the Family

The health of a nation is tied to the health of its families, and strong families are shaped by spiritually healthy churches. Conversely, spiritually grounded churches are built upon spiritually obedient families.

Key Mandates for Strengthening Church and Family Life:

1. Appoint Biblically Qualified Elders *(1 Timothy 3)*

Leaders should model integrity, discipline, and godly leadership in both church and home.

2. Encourage Biblical Headship *(Ephesians 5:23)*

Equip men to lead spiritually, and encourage families to reflect God's divine order in love and mutual honor.

3. Be the Family for the Broken *(Mark 10:30)*

The church must be a refuge and safe haven for the hurting, the fatherless, and the isolated.

RELATIONAL LEADERSHIP IN THE CHURCH

Unlike corporate models of leadership, church leadership is pastoral and relational. Influence in ministry flows from trust, authenticity, and care.

The Shepherd's Role *(John 10)*

Pastors are called to shepherd God's people—to know them, guide them, and protect them. This requires more than Sunday sermons; it demands presence, curiosity, and intentional pursuit.

Practices for Pastoral Connection:
- Ask deeper questions that go beyond surface greetings.
- Learn the names, vocations, and dreams of your congregants.
- Be available in moments of crisis and celebration.
- Lead as a servant, not a celebrity.
- Model vulnerability and grace.

Pastoral curiosity is a spiritual discipline that builds stronger communities.

THE CHURCH AS A TRANSFORMATIONAL COMMUNITY

Community is one of God's greatest gifts to His people. Even in a crowd, we can feel lonely—but the Church is called to be a healing counterculture where true fellowship can flourish.

Four Biblical Reasons Why Community Matters:

1. **Community Encourages** *(Galatians 6:2, Hebrews 10:24–25)*
   We bear each other's burdens and spur one another on in love.

2. **Community Brings Joy** *(Psalm 133:1)*
   Unity is pleasant, powerful, and life-giving.

3. **Community Invites God's Presence** *(Matthew 18:20, Acts 2:46–47)*
   God moves when believers gather in unity, breaking bread with gladness.

4. **Community Fosters Love** *(Colossians 3:13–14)*
   We grow spiritually as we grow relationally—through forgiveness, kindness, and humility.

Whether introverted or outgoing, each believer is called to pursue authentic spiritual connection. It is in the context of real relationships that transformation, healing, and lasting discipleship take place.

We are truly better together.

CASE STUDY: THE EARLY CHURCH MODEL (ACTS 2)

The early church in Acts 2 modeled a radically connected community. They:

- Devoted themselves to teaching and fellowship
- Shared meals and possessions
- Prayed together and worshipped daily
- Gained favor with the wider community

As a result, "the Lord added to their number daily those who were being saved." (Acts 2:47) Their deep relational and spiritual connectedness was the catalyst for explosive, sustainable growth.

FINAL REFLECTIONS

The Church is not merely an institution—it is a relational ecosystem. It thrives when its leaders prioritize connection over charisma, care over control, and presence over performance.

- Invest in the hearts of people.
- Build systems that honor community.
- Be intentional about relational discipleship.

When the church becomes a place where everyone is seen, known, and valued, it reflects the heart of Christ.

PRAYER AND DECLARATION FOR CONNECTEDNESS IN THE CHURCH

Father God,
Thank You for designing us for connection and calling us into community. Let our churches be places of healing, unity, and growth. Give leaders wisdom to shepherd with grace and humility. Let every heart that enters find belonging.
I declare:
> *I will pursue relationships rooted in love and truth.*
> *I will build bridges, not barriers, within the body of Christ.*

> *I will serve with empathy, listen with intention, and lead with compassion.*
> *I will be an instrument of unity, healing, and relational wholeness.*

Make me a vessel for Your love and an ambassador of Your Kingdom.

In Jesus' name, Amen.

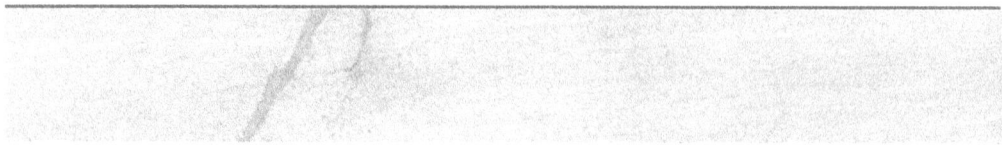

———

ADOPTING A PEOPLE-CENTRIC
APPROACH IN GOVERNANCE

"Do your little bit of good where you are; it's those little bits of good put together that overwhelm the world."

—Desmond Tutu

GOVERNANCE WITH A HIGHER CALLING

I n an age where political systems tremble under the weight of broken trust, and leaders often mistake popularity for purpose, there is a growing cry for governance that heals rather than harms. Governance that listens. Governance that restores. At its core, *people-centric governance* reflects the heart of God—a call to steward nations with justice, mercy, humility, and truth.

The biblical vision for governance is not rooted in domination, but in service. As Isaiah prophesied, "The government shall be upon His shoulders" (Isaiah 9:6), and His rule would be marked by peace, justice, and righteousness. This is a sacred invitation: for leaders to govern not just for the people, but *with* the people, under the weighty accountability of heaven.

GOOD GOVERNANCE AND CITIZEN PARTICIPATION

Smart governance begins with deep listening and radical empathy. It is easy to declare oneself people-centric; much harder to embody it in structures, policies, and practice. When people-centricity is driven by populism or political correctness, the results are often shallow and short-lived.

True people-centric governance is rooted in *dignity, responsibility*, and *empowerment*. It recognizes that governance is not just about institutional performance but about relational trust.

Citizens must see and feel that government action is for them—and ideally, *with* them. When citizens are dignified by the state, they become accountable. When they become accountable, they become responsible. And when responsible citizens participate meaningfully, they contribute to the construction of good governance.

WHY CITIZEN PARTICIPATION MATTERS

Global indicators such as the Worldwide Governance Indicators (WGI) and Asian Development Bank (ADB) frameworks emphasize two indispensable tenets of good governance: **transparency** and **accountability**. Neither is possible without meaningful citizen engagement.

Yet, citizen participation remains elusive in many contexts due to illiteracy, lack of civic education, political naivety, and insufficient engagement platforms. These are not just logistical failures—they are spiritual and moral failures. Governance divorced from participation becomes governance devoid of legitimacy.

To change this narrative, we must:

- Create deliberate platforms for civic voice and agency.
- Strengthen judicial, legislative, and executive mechanisms for inclusive decision-making.
- Promote values-based civic education that develops citizens' sense of responsibility.

As Proverbs 29:2 declares,

"When the righteous are in authority, the people rejoice: but when the wicked beareth rule, the people mourn."

Citizens as Partners: Rebuilding the Trust Bridge

The OECD's *Citizens as Partners* study reminds us that meaningful public participation begins with systemic commitment. Leaders must invest in:

- **Transparent Information**: Objective, relevant, and accessible.
- **Inclusive Consultation**: Honest, wide-reaching dialogue.
- **Empowered Participation**: Creating spaces for shared decision-making.

Nations like Canada, Finland, and Switzerland have taken legislative steps to ensure marginalized voices are not only heard but prioritized. Yet policy alone is insufficient. Leadership matters. As Micah 6:8 instructs, "He has shown you, O man, what is good... to act justly, to love mercy, and to walk humbly with your God."

The Seven "PC" Priorities for People-Centric Policymaking *(Adapted from David Chan's framework)*

1. **Public Concerns**

   True governance distinguishes between *populism* and *public concern*. While populism panders, true leadership discerns both emotional and practical needs and seeks to address them in sustainable ways.

2. **Political Context**

   An engaged citizenry brings vibrant, diverse perspectives. Wise governance fosters innovation through positive political diversity, encouraging communities to co-create solutions.

3. **Policy Content**

   Policies must be holistic, not siloed. They must cohere across sectors, avoiding unintended consequences while enhancing impact.

4. **Policy Communication**

   Good policy must be accompanied by clear, compassionate messaging. Citizens must understand both the intent and the content of governance actions.

5. **Problem-Solving Competence**

   Governments must deliver. Crises should be met with integrity, transparency, and prompt action. Failure to respond erodes public trust and violates the sacred trust of leadership.

6. **Personal Character**

   Trust is earned. People-centric leaders must embody integrity, impartiality, and courage. Character matters more than charisma.

7. **Psychological Capital**

   Governance should inspire hope, resilience, and agency. When people believe they can shape the future, they become builders of nations, not just subjects of policy.

Case Study: Participatory Budgeting
in Porto Alegre, Brazil

One powerful example of people-centric governance in action is the participatory budgeting model pioneered in Porto Alegre, Brazil. Since 1989, the city has invited citizens to directly participate in allocating portions of the municipal budget. Through neighborhood assemblies and thematic committees, citizens propose, debate, and prioritize public investments.

Results have been transformational:

- Improved infrastructure in underserved communities
- Increased citizen satisfaction and political engagement
- Strengthened transparency and reduced corruption

This model has since been replicated globally, proving that when people are trusted with governance, they rise to the occasion. It illustrates the biblical truth that *"plans fail for lack of counsel, but with many advisers they succeed"* (Proverbs 15:22).

Kingdom Governance: Stewarding Nations
with Justice and Compassion

Governance, when rightly understood, is a sacred stewardship. It is not merely about managing resources or enforcing laws; it is about cultivating environments where people can flourish in dignity, peace, and purpose.

The Kingdom model invites leaders to:

- **Lead as Servants** (Matthew 20:26) rather than rulers seeking power.
- **Uphold Justice** for the vulnerable, widows, and orphans (Isaiah 1:17).
- **Govern with Wisdom** that is "pure, peace-loving, considerate, submissive, full of mercy and good fruit" (James 3:17).

This is governance beyond the ballot box. It is leadership anchored in eternity and accountable before God.

Good governance is not just about performance. It is about presence. About showing up for the people. About honouring the image of God in every citizen. It is about recognizing that every policy has a pulse, every system impacts souls, and every decision carries the weight of destiny.

Let the little bits of good begin with listening. Let them multiply through inclusive structures. And let them overwhelm the world through sustained, people-first, Kingdom-rooted transformation.

PRAYER AND DECLARATION FOR KINGDOM LEADERS

Heavenly Father,

We thank You for entrusting leadership and governance into human hands. We acknowledge that all authority belongs to You. Grant our leaders wisdom like Solomon, courage like Esther, and compassion like Jesus. May they govern with integrity, humility, and righteousness.

We declare that:

> *Our nations shall be led by those who fear God and honour truth.*
> *Citizens shall rise in wisdom, responsibility, and prophetic voice.*
> *Corruption shall be uprooted, and justice shall roll like a river.*
> *Governance shall become a conduit of healing, dignity, and hope.*

Raise up a generation of Kingdom-minded leaders who will steward power as a sacred trust and build systems that reflect heaven on earth.

In Jesus' name, Amen.

CHAPTER
NINE

——✠——

NETWORKING SKILLS
FOR LEADERS

"Two are better than one, because they have a good return for their labor."
—Ecclesiastes 4:9

BEYOND CONTACTS: A KINGDOM VIEW OF CONNECTION

In a world saturated with LinkedIn profiles, business cards, and networking events, it's easy to confuse activity with depth. But real networking is not transactional—it is transformational. For Kingdom-minded leaders, networking is not about leveraging others for gain, but stewarding relationships for mutual purpose, impact, and divine alignment.

God designed us for connection. Scripture reminds us that "iron sharpens iron" (Proverbs 27:17) and that where two or three are gathered in His name, He is present (Matthew 18:20). To build networks is not just a leadership practice—it is an expression of Kingdom collaboration and covenantal influence.

NETWORKING: SKILL OR WILL?

Building a leadership network is less a matter of skill than of will. Many leaders abandon networking when initial efforts don't yield immediate rewards, wrongly believing it's a talent they don't possess. But networking, like any other leadership discipline, is developed through intentionality and practice.

Leadership networking involves cultivating relationships and alliances that advance your organization's mission—and often, your personal calling. Done well, it extends influence, unlocks opportunity, and creates spaces for shared wisdom and innovation.

THREE TYPES OF NETWORKING: A STRATEGIC BREAKDOWN

A pivotal 2007 Harvard Business Review study by INSEAD professors Herminia Ibarra and Mark Hunter outlines three essential forms of networking:

1. **Operational Networking**

   These networks focus on relationships that help you perform your current job effectively. They include direct reports, supervisors, peers, customers, and vendors. The goal is coordination and task execution.

However, operational networks tend to be reactive and short-term. They rarely foster the creativity or foresight required for visionary leadership.

2. **Personal Networking**

    These are relationships formed outside one's organization—through alumni groups, associations, faith communities, or mentorship circles. These connections offer perspective, support, and access to new ideas. Though often undervalued in professional spaces, personal networks are essential for resilience, emotional well-being, and leadership longevity.

3. **Strategic Networking**

    This is where transformation begins. Strategic networks connect you to influencers, decision-makers, and visionaries across functions and sectors. They help you:

    - Access new resources
    - Influence beyond your direct authority
    - Align organizational goals with larger movements

Strategic networking is not about visibility for its own sake—it is about Kingdom positioning. Leaders who cultivate such networks anticipate change, shape systems, and lead movements, not just departments.

FROM ISOLATION TO INFLUENCE:
REDEEMING THE NARRATIVE OF NETWORKING

Many Christian or values-driven leaders shy away from networking, fearing it to be self-serving or manipulative. But redeemed networking is deeply biblical. Consider:

- **Joseph**: Rose to influence by faithfully serving in obscurity, interpreting Pharaoh's dream, and managing crisis through relational trust.
- **Esther**: Stewarded her royal position and relationships to save a nation.
- **Nehemiah**: Leveraged favor with the king, mobilized civic resources, and built relational trust among nobles and workers to rebuild Jerusalem.

- **Paul**: Mobilized networks of believers, churches, and collaborators across continents to advance the Gospel.

God uses networks to expand vision and fulfill destiny. The key is to approach networking with humility, clarity, and a servant's heart.

PRACTICAL NETWORKING HABITS FOR KINGDOM LEADERS

- **Pray Before You Connect**: Seek divine alignment, not just opportunity.
- **Serve First**: Ask, "What value can I add?" before "What can I gain?"
- **Follow Up Thoughtfully**: Build consistency and honour time invested.
- **Bridge Circles**: Introduce others who can benefit from each other.
- **Be Authentically You**: Show up with integrity, not performance.

CASE STUDY: THE AFRICAN LEADERSHIP NETWORK (ALN)

The African Leadership Network (ALN) offers a case of networking done with vision and purpose. Formed to connect the continent's most dynamic leaders, ALN fosters relationships that lead to business ventures, social impact collaborations, and policy influence across Africa.

Rather than limiting itself to industry-specific or national boundaries, ALN prioritizes shared values, collective identity, and long-term transformation. Members are encouraged not only to grow their ventures but to invest in each other's dreams. This mirrors the early church: a network of purpose, resource sharing, and mutual upliftment.

FINAL REFLECTIONS

To lead effectively in this generation, one must transcend silos. Whether you're building a start-up, leading a nonprofit, managing a city, or discipling a movement, your ability to cultivate meaningful connections will define your reach and relevance.

Networking isn't about being everywhere—it's about being present, purposeful, and aligned where it truly matters. Kingdom leadership demands networks that are marked not by ambition, but by alignment. Let your networks become ecosystems of mutual growth, wisdom, and generational impact.

Father God,

Thank You for the divine design of connection. Thank You for every relationship You have brought into our lives. Help us discern the people You are calling us to walk with in this season. Teach us to build with integrity, honour, and love.

We declare:

- ⊳ *Our networks shall be filled with purpose, wisdom, and divine timing.*
- ⊳ *We will steward our relationships as gifts, not stepping stones.*
- ⊳ *Our influence shall rise, not by striving, but by divine favour.*
- ⊳ *We shall be connectors, bridge-builders, and carriers of Kingdom vision.*

In Jesus' name, Amen.

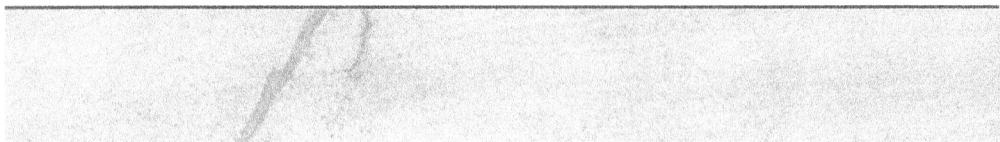

CHAPTER
TEN

—#—

LEADING THROUGH CRISIS
WITH CONNECTION

"When the storms of life come, the wicked are whirled away, but the godly have a lasting foundation."

— Proverbs 10:25 (NLT)

LEADERSHIP IN THE FIRE

Crises are the true crucibles of leadership. They strip away pretense, accelerate exposure, and demand clarity. While some leaders retreat into control, isolation, or fear, Kingdom-minded leaders are called to something higher: connection, courage, and compassionate action.

In moments of crisis—whether organizational upheaval, societal unrest, or personal loss—people don't just need a plan. They need a **presence**. They need leaders who are **anchored, attuned, and available**. Leadership in crisis is less about charisma and more about **calm**. It is not about having all the answers but knowing how to hold space for others while seeking divine guidance.

BIBLICAL MODELS OF CRISIS LEADERSHIP

The Bible is filled with leaders who navigated crisis not by avoiding pressure but by anchoring in connection—first with God, then with people.

- **Nehemiah** faced opposition, exhaustion, and sabotage—yet he *stayed connected to his mission, his team, and his God*. He responded with both strategy and prayer (Nehemiah 4:9).
- **Jesus**, knowing He would face betrayal and the cross, still chose to *wash the disciples' feet*, pray with them, and comfort them (John 13–17).
- **Paul**, imprisoned and uncertain, continued to write, encourage, and connect with churches and fellow believers, demonstrating relational resilience in hardship (Philippians 1:3–6).

Each of these leaders teaches us that **crisis does not break Kingdom leaders—it reveals their foundation**.

THE COST OF DISCONNECTION IN CRISIS

Many leaders, under pressure, default to disconnection. They:

- Withdraw emotionally
- Micro-manage or control
- Suppress vulnerability

- Avoid hard conversations

While understandable, this posture isolates the leader and leaves their team disoriented. Crisis leadership requires intentional **relational alignment**. A disconnected leader leads a fragmented team.

PRINCIPLES FOR LEADING THROUGH CRISIS WITH CONNECTION

1. **Presence Over Performance:**
   People remember how you made them feel, not how perfectly you managed a spreadsheet. Your non-anxious presence becomes a stabilizing force.

   "Even though I walk through the valley of the shadow of death, I will fear no evil, for You are with me."

   —PSALM 23:4

   ---

2. **Communicate Early and Often**
   In crisis, silence breeds fear. Regular, transparent updates—even if incomplete—build trust. Let people know what you know, what you're doing, and how you're processing it.

3. **Lead with Empathy**
   Acknowledge losses, validate feelings, and make space for grief. Empathy connects the leader's heart with the people's reality.

4. **Stay Grounded in Values**
   Decisions made in panic often violate core values. Anchor in what matters most—integrity, faith, compassion, and truth.

5. **Empower Others**
   Crisis leadership is not a solo endeavor. Delegate, elevate, and co-labor. Invite others into responsibility—it builds shared ownership and releases resilience.

Practical Tools for Relational Crisis Leadership

- **Check-in Circles**: Begin meetings with human check-ins before diving into logistics.
- **Prayer or Reflection Pauses**: Invite spiritual grounding into your decision-making.
- **Listening Sessions**: Hold space for your team or community to voice concerns without defense.
- **Visible Availability**: Be seen, be accessible, be interruptible.

Case Study: COVID-19 and Faith-Driven Community Leadership

During the COVID-19 pandemic, many churches and nonprofits became frontline responders—not only offering food and aid, but *relational connection in the midst of chaos*. One community leader in South Africa mobilized a WhatsApp prayer and resource network that kept thousands connected across isolation. The secret? Not high-tech strategy, but **relational intentionality**— consistent communication, shared faith, and communal care.

This reflects a truth for every crisis: **the strength of your relationships determines the strength of your response**.

FINAL REFLECTIONS

Crisis will come. But the kind of leader you become in the fire will determine what emerges on the other side. If you lead from fear, you may survive. But if you lead from connection, you will help others *heal, grow, and rebuild*.

Let your leadership in crisis reflect the **God who never leaves nor forsakes us**, even in the storm. And may your relationships be your greatest resource—not your last resort.

Father, God,

Thank You for being a refuge in times of trouble. You are our anchor when the winds rage. Raise up leaders who do not crumble in crisis, but stand as bridges of peace, pillars of strength, and vessels of compassion.

We declare:

> *We shall not lead from fear, but from faith and connection.*

> *Our teams and communities shall be bound by trust and not torn by panic.*

> *We shall speak words of life, truth, and clarity in times of uncertainty.*

> *We shall mirror the heart of Christ—present, wise, and full of grace.*

We receive Your courage, Your wisdom, and Your presence for every crisis ahead. In Jesus' name, Amen.

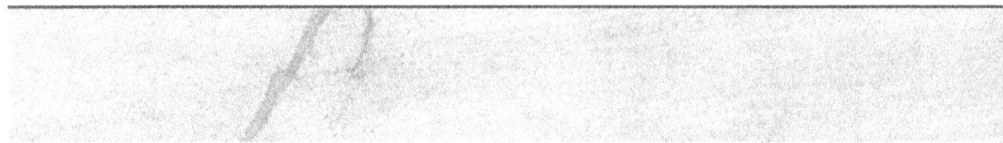

CHAPTER

ELEVEN

—‖—

THE LEGACY
OF RELATIONAL LEADERSHIP

"And the things you have heard me say in the presence of many witnesses,
entrust to reliable people who will also be qualified to teach others."

— 2 Timothy 2:2 (NIV)

LEGACY IS RELATIONAL, NOT JUST POSITIONAL

T itles fade. Strategies evolve. Organizations change. But relationships endure—and multiply. The true legacy of leadership is not what you build *for* people but what you deposit *in* people.

Relational leadership is legacy leadership. It recognizes that every conversation, every act of trust, every moment of mentorship becomes a seed sown into eternity. It's not about how widely you are known, but how deeply others are transformed by encountering your life and leadership.

In the Kingdom, legacy is not measured in accolades but in disciples, successors, and sons and daughters—those who carry the vision further than you ever could.

BIBLICAL MODELS OF LEGACY LEADERSHIP

The Scriptures are filled with legacy-minded leaders who poured themselves into others:

- **Moses prepared Joshua**, not just to continue a mission, but to lead with courage and presence (Deuteronomy 31:7–8).
- **Elijah passed the mantle to Elisha**, and Elisha performed double the miracles—not because of strategy, but relationship (2 Kings 2).
- **Jesus spent most of His time with 12**, not 12,000. He knew that depth produces multiplication.
- **Paul mentored Timothy and Titus**, leaving behind not just letters, but spiritual sons and apostolic leaders (1 Timothy 1:2).

Each of these leaders had this in common: they lived and led *beyond themselves*.

WHAT ARE YOU REALLY PASSING ON?

A legacy is always being written—whether intentionally or accidentally. Every leader must wrestle with these questions:

- Will my leadership outlive my position?
- Am I building systems or building people?

- Do those closest to me feel empowered or used?
- Have I created pathways for others to rise?

The power of relational legacy is that it transfers not just knowledge, but DNA—vision, character, conviction, and calling. It leaves a mark on hearts, not just headlines.

RELATIONAL LEGACY IN ACTION: BEYOND MENTORSHIP

To build a relational legacy, you must do more than teach. You must **invest, impart, and empower**.

1. **Invest Time Intentionally**

   Legacy is not microwaved. It's brewed slowly through consistent presence, listening, and doing life together.

2. **2. Impart Values, Not Just Vision**

   Help others grasp the *why* behind the *what*. Share your wins and your wounds. Vulnerability deepens legacy.

3. **Empower Through Trust**

   Give people real responsibility. Let them lead. Let them fail. Let them grow.

As John Maxwell says,

"Success is when those who know you best respect you the most."

CASE STUDY: AFRICA'S EMERGING GENERATIONAL MOVEMENTS

Across the African continent, new movements of leadership are being birthed—not from boardrooms alone, but from living rooms, coffee conversations, and intergenerational connections.

From faith communities to business incubators, young leaders are being discipled by seasoned voices who are willing to walk closely—not just speak from platforms. Organizations like **The Emerging Leaders Foundation (Kenya)** and **Ziwani (South Africa)** are showing that sustainable transformation is not driven by charisma—but by **intentional legacy-building** relationships.

Practical Ways to Cultivate Legacy

- **Identify your successors now**—not later. Invite them to shadow, share, and shape with you.
- **Document your journey**—write, record, or share your lessons and stories.
- **Champion others publicly**—honour, promote, and affirm those around you.
- **Build leadership pipelines**, not pedestals.
- **Leave relational "wills"**—write letters, pray blessings, or record personal messages to those you've mentored.

Legacy is not left by chance. It is built by design.

FINAL REFLECTIONS

Your greatest legacy won't be your resume—it will be the people who rise because you believed in them. Relational leadership doesn't just build movements. It births *generations*.

So, as you reflect on your own journey, ask yourself: *Who am I raising? Who will carry what God has entrusted to me?*

Let your leadership echo in those you've poured into. Let your legacy be a living lineage of leaders who lead with love, truth, and transformation.

PRAYER AND DECLARATION FOR GENERATIONAL IMPACT

Lord God,

Thank You for calling us to lead not only in this generation, but for the sake of those to come. You are the God of Abraham, Isaac, and Jacob—You think generationally. Let our leadership be rooted in that same mindset.

We declare:

> ⊳ *We will not hoard wisdom—we will pass it on with grace and humility.*
> ⊳ *We will raise leaders who surpass us, honour You, and steward well.*
> ⊳ *Our lives will not end with applause, but with impact that outlives us.*
> ⊳ *Our legacy will not be built on ego, but on intentional relationships and eternal seeds.*

May we live and lead with heaven in view—and generations in mind.
In Jesus' name, Amen.

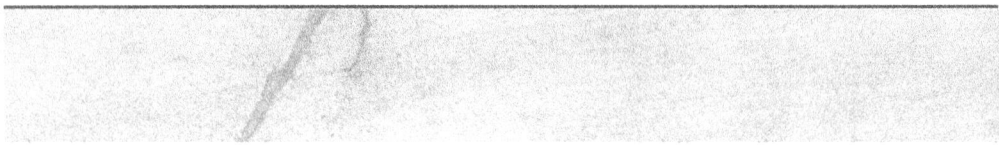

TWELVE

—‖—

WHOLENESS
AS A LEADERSHIP PRACTICE

"Beloved, I pray that you may prosper in all things and be in health,
just as your soul prospers."

—3 JOHN 1:2 (NKJV)

LEADERSHIP THAT FLOWS FROM THE INSIDE OUT

In a world that glorifies productivity and performance, the inner life of a leader is often neglected—until it breaks. We applaud outcomes, celebrate metrics, and chase milestones... while quietly ignoring exhaustion, emotional disconnection, or spiritual dryness.

But there is a better way.

Wholeness is not a luxury for leaders—it is a **necessity**. Because when leaders lead from fullness, they give from overflow, not depletion. They steward power with peace. They cast vision without being crushed by it.

Wholeness is the foundation of sustainable leadership.

WHAT IS WHOLENESS?

Wholeness is not perfection. It is the pursuit of alignment—across spirit, soul, body, and relationships. It is when your identity, values, actions, and vision move in rhythm rather than conflict.

Whole leaders:
- Know who they are apart from what they do
- Nurture rest, reflection, and restoration
- Set boundaries that protect calling and capacity
- Seek healing for past wounds and embrace emotional maturity
- Lead with presence, not pressure

BIBLICAL MODELS OF WHOLE LEADERSHIP

- **David**, despite his flaws, consistently returned to God for soul restoration: *"He restores my soul"* (Psalm 23:3).
- **Jesus** modeled rhythm—teaching, healing, then withdrawing to solitary places to pray (Luke 5:16).
- **Elijah**, after burnout, was restored by God through rest, nourishment, and renewed purpose (1 Kings 19).
- **Joseph**, even after betrayal and imprisonment, led with grace and

reconciliation—proof that emotional healing fuels redemptive leadership.

Their lives remind us that God does not just anoint leaders—He heals them.

Why Many Leaders Struggle with Wholeness

- The **tyranny of urgency** crowds out the inner life.
- Fear of appearing weak prevents leaders from seeking support.
- Systems reward output over sustainability.
- Cultural narratives glorify burnout as a badge of honour.

But the cost is steep: relational breakdowns, moral failure, depression, disillusionment, spiritual numbness. Leaders cannot afford to lead disconnected from their core.

Practicing Wholeness: Rhythms of Renewal

1. **Retreat and Reflection**

   Regularly withdraw to reset. Journal. Ask:
   - What am I carrying that God never asked me to?
   - Where am I misaligned in thought, emotion, or energy?

2. **Spiritual Nourishment**

   Feed your spirit through prayer, worship, and the Word—not just as rituals, but relational nourishment.

3. **Therapy and Mentorship**

   Healing is holy. Emotional wounds affect leadership. Seek out wise counselors and mentors who carry both grace and truth.

4. **Body Stewardship**

   Your body is the temple of the Holy Spirit. Rest, hydration, exercise, and Sabbath are not optional—they are spiritual disciplines.

5. **Healthy Relational Boundaries**

Lead with love, not codependency. Say yes with clarity, and no with peace. Protect your emotional and spiritual margin.

WHOLENESS IS A LEADERSHIP WITNESS

When leaders walk in wholeness, they model Kingdom living. They teach their teams that rest is not laziness. That vulnerability is not weakness. That integrity and alignment matter more than applause.

A whole leader builds healthy teams, safe cultures, and visionary movements that endure.

FINAL REFLECTIONS

You were never created to lead from burnout, brokenness, or bravado. You were designed to lead from the overflow of wholeness.

Let your leadership be a living witness—that it is possible to be *strong and soft, visionary and grounded, influential and at peace.*

This is your charge: **Lead with your whole heart. Serve from your whole soul. Build with your whole mind. Love with your whole strength.** That is the essence of Kingdom leadership.

PRAYER AND DECLARATION FOR WHOLENESS IN LEADERSHIP

Father,

Creator of all wholeness, You have not called us to strive, but to abide. You have not asked us to burn out in Your name, but to burn brightly with Your love.

Heal every wound that hinders our leadership. Realign our hearts with Your rhythm. Restore what stress, grief, and fear have stolen.

We declare:

- ▷ *We are not defined by what we produce, but by whose we are.*
- ▷ *We will live and lead from a place of joy, not just responsibility.*
- ▷ *Our decisions will flow from discernment, not depletion.*

▷ *Our legacy will be rooted in peace, integrity, and emotional maturity.*

We surrender performance for presence, pressure for purpose, and ambition for alignment.

May our leadership reflect the wholeness of the One who called us. In Jesus' name, Amen.

A PRAYER FOR LEADERS, BUILDERS, AND KINGDOM COLLABORATORS

Mighty God,

Thank You for entrusting me with vision. Thank You for reminding me that the call upon my life will never be fulfilled in isolation, but through covenantal partnerships and divine alignments.

Lord, open my eyes to see the builders You have sent. Sharpen my discernment to know who to walk with, when to let go, and how to steward every relationship with integrity and honour.

Teach me to lead with humility, to serve with excellence, and to collaborate with purpose. Guard my heart from pride, offence, and comparison. Let my leadership be marked by grace, wisdom, and mutual respect.

May the partnerships I form advance Your kingdom, reflect Your love, and leave a legacy of impact that outlives me. Strengthen me to lead in connection, not competition—and to walk boldly into the strategic relationships You've prepared for me.

In Jesus' Name,

Amen.

THE CONNECTION FACTOR SERIES

This powerful series by Cynthia Chirinda explores the transformative power of authentic connection—starting from self-awareness and extending to strategic alliances. Titles in the series include:

1. **The Connection Factor for Personal Growth**
   Unlocking Your True Potential Through Meaningful Relationships
   A guide to connecting with yourself and others across personal, professional, and spiritual spheres. Offers practical wisdom for auditing, nurturing, or recalibrating relationships for holistic growth.

2. **The Connection Factor for Women**
   Unlock the Power of Purposeful Connections
   A strategic guide for women to build authentic engagement, overcome relational barriers, and cultivate networks that accelerate growth and legacy-building.

3. **The Connection Factor for Leaders**
   Unlocking Value from Your Strategic Partners
   A relational leadership handbook for qualifying, auditing, and aligning stakeholder relationships for long-term impact and organizational purpose.

Each book in the series is designed to stand alone while weaving together one core truth:
We were never meant to walk alone.
Your growth, purpose, and legacy are nurtured through intentional, life-giving connections.

ABOUT THE AUTHOR

Cynthia Chirinda is a Transformation Catalyst, Systems Change Practitioner, and Personal Development Coach committed to helping individuals and institutions thrive in purpose-driven alignment. Her work bridges faith, leadership, and human development across diverse sectors—from grassroots communities to policy tables.

Through her writing, speaking, and coaching work, Cynthia continues to champion authentic connection as the foundation for wholeness, influence, and impact.

She is the author of several life-shaping books, including:
- *The Connection Factor Series* (Personal Growth, Women, Leaders)
- *Can the Whole Woman Please Stand Up!*
- *Managing Transitions: Navigating Change with Grace*
- *The Whole You—Vital Keys for Balanced Living*
- *Destination Wholeness—Going Beyond Brokenness*
- *You Are Not Damaged Goods* series (*Reboot and Start Afresh, Blossom and Flourish, Transitioning from Tragedies to Triumph*)
- *Clothed By Love*
- *The Wealthy Diary of African Wisdom*
- *Intelligent Conversations—A Mindset Shift Towards a Developed Africa*
- *Whole Enough to Go: Embracing God's Call in Imperfection*

Co-authored works: *Success Within Reach, Reinvented and Victorious: The Anthology*

She is also the visionary behind:

- **Intelligent Conversations with Cynthia**—a transformative broadcast platform for leadership and healing dialogues
- **Women Rising in Africa**—a multimedia series spotlighting women leaders across the continent
- **The Extra Mile**—a documentary tribute to women building nations through courage and faith

Wholeness is not about perfection—it is about courageously embracing each season, becoming rooted in faith, and rising into God-ordained purpose.

Connect with Cynthia:
Website: www.cynthiachirinda.com
Email: info@cynthiachirinda.com
LinkedIn: Cynthia Chirinda

www.ingramcontent.com/pod-product-compliance
Lightning Source LLC
Chambersburg PA
CBHW071608200326
41519CB00021BB/6917